CW01513006

Original title:
Wheaten Pollen Beside the Fae Stack

Author: Paula Raudsepp
ISBN HARDBACK: 978-1-80562-069-3
ISBN PAPERBACK: 978-1-80563-590-1

Dappled Sunshine and Whimsical Whispers

In golden light, the shadows play,
Soft whispers dance, where children sway.
Leaves quiver gently in the breeze,
Nature's secrets, the heart's keys.

Fairies at Dusk

As twilight drapes the world in charm,
Soft figures flit, spreading warmth like balm.
Beneath the stars, they laugh and twirl,
In silken dreams, they freely swirl.

Hidden in Gold

Amidst the fields of emerald green,
Lies a treasure, seldom seen.
Golden grains in a soft breeze sway,
Whispers of secrets, come what may.

The Dance of Pollination's Whisper

Bees hum softly, the flowers sigh,
Under the vast and azure sky.
Petals open, a vibrant show,
In nature's dance, the magic flows.

Celestial Moments in the Field's Heart

In the quiet of the evening glow,
Stars awaken, their magic grows.
Fields breathe deep, in stillness found,
Nature's heartbeat, a soothing sound.

Enigma Wrapped in Amber Stalks

In fields where shadows softly blend,
Amber stalks whisper tales untold,
Secrets of the past they send,
From roots that cradle dreams of gold.

Glimmers dance beneath the sun,
Each leaf a memory, well-preserved,
Time seems to halt, a web begun,
In nature's gaze, the heart is stirred.

Winds carry laughter through the space,
While echoes linger in the air,
Beneath that weathered, sun-kissed face,
Each pulse a story, rich and rare.

A riddle wrapped in nature's skin,
The earth beneath our longing feet,
Unraveling with every spin,
As dusk invites the stars to greet.

In twilight's hush, the night reveals,
The mysteries of the amber beds,
With each new dawn, the heart appeals,
To secrets cradled in their threads.

The Eldritch Call of Twilight Meadows

Beneath the moonlight's silken veil,
Twilight meadows breathe a sigh,
Echoes of whispers, in the pale,
Where secrets wander, shy and spry.

A flicker on the edge of dreams,
Shadows mold into soft delight,
With every rustle, magic seems,
To pulse beneath the watchful night.

Stars above bear witness keen,
To stories woven in the mist,
Nature's canvas, vibrant, green,
Where every moment feels like bliss.

The air is thick with ancient lore,
A tapestry of life unfolds,
Calling forth what once was more,
In chilling touch, the heart beholds.

As night enfolds the waking land,
The eldritch call begins to sing,
With delicate grace, it takes your hand,
In meadows where the shadows cling.

Echoes of the Harvested Heart

In ripened fields where laughter grew,
The scent of grain hangs in the air,
Each stalk a dream of sunlit hue,
A memory captured, bittersweet and rare.

The autumn breeze plays soft and low,
In whispers that the spirits send,
Ghosts of harvest, ebb and flow,
With every sigh, they twist and bend.

Gathered shadows of the past,
Reminders of the love once sown,
In every heartbeat, echoes cast,
Of souls who walked this ground alone.

As twilight spills its gentle light,
And stars awaken from their sleeps,
The heart reflects in quiet night,
In echoes where the harvest keeps.

Through swollen fields, the shadows dart,
Each corner holds a tale of worth,
A tapestry woven, the harvested heart,
Is bound to the secrets of the earth.

A Tangle of Green and Gold

In twilight's grip, a tangle grows,
Where emerald leaves meet gilded rays,
A hidden world that nature knows,
In whispered tones, the wild heart plays.

The sun dips low, a fierce embrace,
Illuminating paths before,
Within the branches, life finds grace,
As shadows dance on nature's floor.

Golden threads weave stories twined,
Each rustle tells of time gone by,
In every leaf, a fate aligned,
As morning's dew begins to dry.

The colors clash in vibrant hues,
A symphony of earth and sky,
Where nature sings their timeless blues,
And dreams entwine as hours fly.

In tangled joy, the heart will seek,
The secrets held in nature's fold,
In every rustle, every peak,
A dance of life, both green and gold.

Where Shadows Play in the Golds

In fields where whispers touch the air,
Golden light does dance with flair.
Shadows cast by ancient trees,
Sing tales lost in summer's breeze.

Beneath the boughs, the secrets hide,
Where gentle rustlings' echoes bide.
A world of wonder, soft and sweet,
A wayward heart finds its heartbeat.

Sunrays filter through leafy guise,
Painting dreams where magic lies.
With every flutter, new paths unfold,
In silent stories, the past is told.

The air is thick with scents divine,
Of nectar sweet and wilding vine.
In these quiet moments, we play,
And capture time in shades of gray.

So linger long by nature's side,
Let instinct's pull be your guide.
For in the grove where shadows sway,
True joy emerges, come what may.

Secrets Cradled in Rustling Leaves

Among the branches, secrets dwell,
In whispers soft, they weave their spell.
The rustling leaves, a gentle sigh,
Hiding tales of days gone by.

Sunlight dapples as shadows play,
Casting dreams on the ground's array.
The winds carry lore, old and wise,
Inviting us to dream and rise.

Each gust reveals a story bound,
In nature's verse, where truths abound.
The tree trunks stand, steadfast and tall,
Guardians of secrets shared by all.

Mysterious paths twist and twine,
With magic woven, twinkling divine.
Under the canopy, hearts ignite,
In labyrinths kissed by golden light.

Let us wander through wild and free,
Listening closely, you and me.
For in the rustle, spirits align,
In harmony, both yours and mine.

The Weaving of Sunlight and Folklore

In dawning light, the stories bloom,
Weaving threads in nature's loom.
Sunbeams dance on emerald blades,
Bringing forth life's vibrant shades.

Folklore twirls on a zephyr's breath,
From ancient tales defying death.
The birds chant songs of times before,
Echoes of lore that we adore.

Beneath the sky, a canvas vast,
Infinite dreams from ages past.
Each petal and leaf spins a tale,
Of nightingale's song and evening's veil.

In the woods, the spirits tread,
Where legends linger, softly spread.
With every heartbeat, tales we share,
Binding us close in whispered air.

So grab your dreams and lift them high,
With every twinkle of the sky.
For in the weaving of light and lore,
We find our way forevermore.

Dreams Brewed in Nature's Cauldron

In nature's cauldron, dreams take flight,
A bubbling brew of day and night.
With twigs and leaves, we stir the pot,
Creating visions, weaving thought.

The fragrance of earth and skies combine,
In this enchanted space, divine.
Stars awaken in the twilight's glow,
Whispers of magic begin to flow.

Winds whisper secrets, old yet new,
Crafting spells for hearts so true.
With each heartbeat, a pulse we share,
In this cauldron, dreams lay bare.

The moonlit paths beckon us near,
While fireflies twinkle, pure and clear.
In the embrace of midnight's song,
Nature calls, where we belong.

So gather 'round this mystical tool,
With wonders ablaze, we break the rule.
For in this cauldron, fate's brew does spin,
Awakening the dreams within.

Tales of the Verdant Hollow

In the heart where shadows reel,
Whispers echo, secrets steal.
Trees entwined in emerald grace,
A hidden realm, a magic place.

Beneath the boughs, the fae do dance,
With twinkling eyes, their fleeting glance.
Mossy carpets, soft as dreams,
Where nothing's ever as it seems.

Brooks gurgle tales of ancient days,
In vibrant tones, through leafy maze.
Nests of feathers, whispers low,
Stories only nature knows.

Moonlight spills on petals bright,
Casting shadows in the night.
Within the hollow, shadows play,
Guarding secrets day by day.

So gather close, and lean in near,
Let the tales draw you near.
For every leaf, a story spun,
In the hollow, magic's begun.

Nectar of the Sun-kissed Earth

Golden rays on dew-kissed grass,
Whispering winds of summer's pass.
Blossoms bloom with colors bright,
Gifting joy in morning light.

Bees hum softly, busy and wise,
Dancing under painted skies.
Nectar sweet, a life's embrace,
Nature's love in every place.

Windswept meadows, laughter's song,
An ode to life, forever strong.
Rippling fields of green and gold,
Stories of the earth retold.

With every step, the petals sigh,
Embracing moments passing by.
In the fragrance, dreams arise,
A paradise beneath the skies.

So sip the nectar, let it flow,
Awaken dreams we long to know.
In sun-kissed earth, we find our worth,
A symphony of nature's mirth.

Luminescence Laced with Lore

Stars alight on velvet deep,
Guardians of the dreams we keep.
With every flicker, histories weave,
In whispers soft, the night believes.

Moonlit paths through ancient trees,
Echoes dance upon the breeze.
Woven tales of love and fate,
Every spark, a tale innate.

Constellations, bright and bold,
Crafting stories long retold.
Galaxies swirl with secrets lost,
A glimmered path through time's frost.

As shadows grow, the night unfolds,
In the stillness, magic molds.
Every heartbeat, a tale to share,
In luminescence, dreams lay bare.

So gaze upon the skies above,
Feel the warmth of a starlit love.
In every glimmer, lore ignites,
A journey spun in starry nights.

The Hidden Garden's Heartbeat

Within the walls of tangled vines,
A hidden garden pulses, shines.
With petals soft and colors bold,
Whispers of the earth unfold.

The heartbeat of the blooms resounds,
In secret paths, magic abounds.
Glistening dew on leaves awake,
Nature's breath, a gentle quake.

Butterflies flutter, bright and free,
Painted wonders, a sight to see.
Each blossom bends in sweet embrace,
Creating harmony in space.

Sunlight dapples the fragrant air,
Enchantments linger everywhere.
A tapestry of life we weave,
In every moment, we believe.

So step with care, let your heart feel,
The rhythm of the garden's reel.
For in each corner, wild and true,
Beats the wisdom of the dew.

Chronicles of the Verdant Enclave

In a realm where whispers weave,
Lush green canopies dance and breathe.
Mystery cloaked in emerald hues,
Secrets told by the morning dews.

Beneath the boughs, old tales unfurl,
Of hidden fae and gems that swirl.
Each petal soft, each branch a scribe,
Recording life in nature's vibe.

Through tangled roots, an ancient song,
Calls to wanderers, brave and strong.
The moonlit nights bring dreams to bare,
As starlit paths begin to share.

When shadows play at the edge of light,
Magic twinkles in the shroud of night.
In every rustle, in every sigh,
The enclave's heart begins to fly.

Harmony blooms in every heart,
From every soul, a vibrant part.
In the verdant folds, we find our grace,
United here, in nature's embrace.

The Sway of the Enchanted Grove

In a grove where silence sways,
Time drifts gently through sunlit rays.
Leaves murmur secrets, soft and low,
As twilight weaves its golden glow.

The branches arch, a welcoming frame,
As woodland creatures join the game.
A dance of shadows, light and shade,
In nature's stage, our fears allayed.

With every step on mossy floor,
The heartbeats echo, evermore.
A whispering breeze through ancient pines,
Invites the soul to draw the lines.

Beneath the stars in velvet skies,
We find our dreams in firefly eyes.
Together bound by earth and sky,
In this enchanted grove, we sigh.

A lullaby sung by the night,
Guides lost travelers to the light.
With every sway, the grove persists,
In magic's hold, we shall exist.

Rhythms of the Rustic Realm

In fields where laughter fills the air,
Golden crops sway without a care.
The rustic charm of everyday,
Paints our lives in warm array.

The brook sings soft, a gentle tune,
Beneath the gaze of watchful moon.
Each rhythm found in nature's breath,
Life pulses on, defying death.

With every dawn, a canvas clear,
Brush-strokes made of love and cheer.
We gather 'round the fire's glow,
Sharing stories that ebb and flow.

A patchwork quilt of life we sew,
Through trials faced, we learn and grow.
Each season brings a new delight,
In rustic lands, our spirits light.

Here, among the hills and streams,
Nature cradles all our dreams.
The rhythm of this realm we feel,
In every pulse, our hearts conceal.

Softly Falling from Nature's Cleft

From nature's cleft, the petals fall,
Each whispering breeze, a tender call.
A dance of colors, sweetly spun,
In every blossom, life's begun.

The forest floor, a patchwork made,
Of shifting shadows, soft and played.
In every crevice, life will find,
A gentle touch, both brave and kind.

With morning's light, the critters stir,
Their joyous songs in sweet demur.
A canopy of life unfurls,
In nature's arms, a treasure hurls.

Softly falling, teardrops trace,
The silent beauty of this place.
Where moments linger, time stands still,
In nature's cleft, we find our will.

A tapestry of earth and sky,
Awaits the dreamer with a sigh.
In every leaf, in every sigh,
Life softly falls, as we comply.

The Sprite's Lament in the Field

In moonlit meadows, shadows dance,
The sprite laments her lost romance.
With gentle sighs, the breezes weep,
Her heart, a secret she must keep.

The flowers nod in sweet despair,
As starlit tears fall through the air.
Each petal whispers tales untold,
Of love and dreams, now lost and cold.

The dew-kissed grass remembers still,
The laughter that once graced the hill.
Yet time, it wanders, soft yet cruel,
A fading echo, a broken jewel.

Beneath the arch of sky so vast,
She weeps for love that could not last.
Glimmers of hope in night's embrace,
Yet haunted still by empty space.

In twilight's arms, where wishes wane,
The sprite remains, a ghost of pain.
Yet in her heart, a glimmer glows,
A tale of love that ever flows.

Ephemeral Dreams in Amber Light

Beneath a sky of amber hue,
The dreams of dusk come drifting through.
With whispered hopes and heart's delight,
They spin like fireflies through the night.

In fleeting moments, shadows play,
As sunlight fades to end the day.
With every breath, a wish takes flight,
In ephemeral dreams, pure and bright.

The twilight sings, a lullaby,
As stars awaken in the sky.
Each shimmering spark, a promise made,
In golden light, our fears will fade.

The world is hushed, the magic near,
In amber warmth, we lose our fear.
For in this time, the heart can soar,
To chase the dreams we long for more.

As darkness falls, we'll hold on tight,
To memories forged in amber light.
Though moments fade, they leave a trace,
Of love that time cannot erase.

Rustic Whispers of the Earth

In fields of green, the whispers flow,
From ancient roots, the stories grow.
The earth, it breathes in gentle sighs,
Beneath the vast and watchful skies.

With every stone and bending tree,
A tapestry of history.
Rustic secrets wrapped in the moss,
Tell tales of gain, of love, of loss.

The river's song, a soothing balm,
It murmurs softly, sweet and calm.
Each ripple holds a memory dear,
Of laughter shared throughout the year.

In twilight's glow, the shadows blend,
With nature's heart, our souls will mend.
For in the whispers of the earth,
We find the magic of our birth.

So linger close, and heed the call,
Of rustic leaves that gently fall.
In every breath, let nature's grace,
Embrace your heart in warm embrace.

Fluttering Beneath the Verdant Canopy

Beneath the boughs, where shadows weave,
The whispers of the forest grieve.
With every flutter, wings take flight,
In nature's arms, a pure delight.

The leaves above, a tapestry,
Of emerald hues, wild and free.
As sunbeams dance on dewy glades,
The magic of the forest fades.

In secret nooks, the fairies play,
With laughter echoing all the way.
Their giggles rise like morning mist,
In every moment, love persists.

The ferns unfurl in gentle trust,
Drawing strength from earth and dust.
In every corner, life abounds,
With fluttering joy in sacred grounds.

So wander forth, let spirits soar,
In verdant dreams forevermore.
For in these woods, with heart aligned,
You'll find the treasures long defined.

Tales from the Breezy Glade

In the glade where shadows dance,
Whispers tell of ancient chance.
Leaves murmur tales of times gone by,
Beneath the watchful, shimmering sky.

With each breeze, a story flows,
Of hidden paths where magic glows.
Creatures stir in twilight's embrace,
Guardians of this secret place.

Stars peek through the leafy quilt,
A tapestry of dreams unbuilt.
Hope hangs like dew on fragile thread,
In this haven where fears are shed.

Echoes linger, soft and clear,
Every laugh, a note to hear.
In this realm where lost things find,
A glimmer of the heart and mind.

So tread lightly, for here you see,
The magic of what's meant to be.
Nature's song will guide your way,
In the Breezy Glade we play.

Midsummer's Glow in the Tall Grass

Golden sunlight spills like wine,
Through the blades where shadows twine.
In the fields where whispers creep,
The tall grass sways, a secret keep.

Dancing lightly, fireflies gleam,
Painting the dusk with fleeting dream.
The crickets sing as night takes hold,
In echoes soft, their stories told.

The warmth of day begins to fade,
Leaving trails in the cool cascade.
Where laughter lingers, hearts grow bold,
In magic woven, like threads of gold.

Beneath the stars, the world feels right,
As moonbeams shimmer with silver light.
In the tall grass, lovers roam,
Finding joy, their hearts a home.

Midsummer's eve, a cherished hour,
Embrace the magic, bask in power.
For in this glow, all troubles cease,
In the tall grass, we find our peace.

Secret Lives of the Wildflowers

In the quiet where petals curl,
Wildflowers bloom, a vibrant swirl.
Each hue speaks in whispers soft,
Stories hidden, dreams aloft.

From roots buried deep in the earth,
They rise to greet the sun's rebirth.
Dancing lightly in the breeze,
Their laughter carried with such ease.

In the morning's light, they open wide,
Bathed in dew, with nothing to hide.
Each blossom knows it plays a role,
In nature's grand, unyielding scroll.

Secrets shared by bumblebees,
Whispers floating on gentle trees.
In this world where colors blend,
The wildflowers weave tales without end.

So pause a moment, take a glance,
At lives unfolding in a dance.
For in their simple, quiet grace,
Lies the magic of this place.

Enchanted Breezes and Golden Fields

Golden fields stretch far and wide,
Where dreams and laughter take their ride.
Enchanted breezes through the grain,
Whisper secrets, joy, and pain.

Beneath the sky, a canvas bright,
Bathed in warmth, embracing light.
Each gentle gust a story spun,
Binding hearts 'til daylight's done.

Bring your hopes to this vast sea,
Feel the freedom, let it be.
Nature's breath, a sweet delight,
In every moment, pure and right.

As twilight descends, hues transform,
The fields take on a dreamy form.
And in the dusk, a magic grows,
In every blade, a secret shows.

So journey forth where visions call,
In golden fields, we rise and fall.
Enchanted breezes guide your heart,
In this cherished realm, we shall never part.

Serenade of the Swaying Stalks

In the quiet dusk they sway,
Softly dancing, come what may.
Whispers carried on the breeze,
Nature's song among the trees.

Golden grains like laughter sing,
Rustling under autumn's wing.
Every stalk a tale unfolds,
Of magic past and futures bold.

Moonlight bathes the field in glow,
Casting shadows, ebb and flow.
Beneath a tapestry of stars,
Dreams take flight, where hope marrs.

Gentle rhythm, sweet embrace,
Earth's own heart in sacred place.
Through the night the symphony,
Plays a ballad wild and free.

Breathing Life into the Fields

Upon the canvas lush and wide,
Nature's pulse we shall abide.
With every seed, a wish is sown,
In fragrant soil life is grown.

Sunrise paints the land in gold,
Whispers of the earth retold.
Roots entwine beneath the ground,
In silence, miracles abound.

Dewdrops glisten like bright stars,
Awakening the earth from scars.
Every blade a testament,
To endless life, our hearts cement.

Carried on a zephyr's wing,
The song of nature starts to sing.
Resilience blooms in every hue,
An ode to all that's bright and true.

Whiffs of Wonder Within the Thicket

In the thicket where shadows play,
Secrets linger, hint and sway.
Mossy stones and twisted vines,
Guard the tales of ancient signs.

A tapestry of green unfolds,
Each rustling leaf a story holds.
Sweet scents wafting on the air,
Nature's wonders, rich and rare.

Dappled light through branches falls,
Gentle laughter sweetly calls.
Crickets chirp their evening song,
Joining where the wild things throng.

A hidden world where dreams take flight,
In shadows deep, there shines a light.
Every wanderer finds a muse,
In the thicket, heart to choose.

Alchemy of the Artisan's Hands

In the glow of twilight's grace,
Tools of wonder find their place.
With every stroke, a spell is cast,
From humble clay, futures amassed.

Molded dreams in fingers dance,
Crafted beauty, given chance.
Chisels whisper, tears of stone,
Sculpting visions, all their own.

Colors twirl in vibrant bliss,
A painter's heart, a swirled kiss.
From brush to canvas, stories flow,
In every corner, magic grows.

An artisan's call, bold and true,
Weaving worlds in strokes of hue.
In crafted realms, the heart expands,
For wonder springs from skilled hands.

Golden Grains Whispering Secrets

In fields where golden grains do sway,
The whispers of the wind convey.
Each stalk a tale, a secret spun,
Beneath the warmth of the setting sun.

The farmer's hands, with tender care,
Tend to the earth, a bond so rare.
Roots delve deep in ancient lore,
Harvesting dreams from the fertile floor.

The harvest moon casts silver light,
Bathing the fields in a glow so bright.
Listen close, for they gently sigh,
Sharing the wisdom of days gone by.

From dew-kissed morn to twilight's fade,
The heart of nature's serenade.
Each grain a story, each breeze a song,
In this embrace, we all belong.

In twilight's glow, the shadows dance,
As night descends, the stars entrance.
Golden grains, your secrets flow,
In whispered dreams, forever grow.

Enchantment Beneath the Meadow's Embrace

In meadows lush where flowers bloom,
An enchanted world dispels the gloom.
Petals whisper what winds have heard,
Nature sings in colors stirred.

Beneath the boughs of ancient trees,
The melodies float upon the breeze.
With every footfall, magic stirs,
In the quiet hum of nature's purrs.

The stream that dances, the stones that gleam,
Craft stories woven like a dream.
In patches soft, the fae do play,
Underneath the moon's gentle sway.

Wildflowers paint as if by spell,
Secrets held in each petal's swell.
The meadow whispers, lush and wide,
A sanctuary where spirits bide.

When twilight beckons, shadows creep,
The enchantment deepens, secrets keep.
In every rustle and tranquil sigh,
Lives a magic that won't pass by.

Threads of Nature's Silken Dance

In nature's loom, the threads entwine,
Woven whispers in emerald line.
Each leaf a story, each bloom a note,
Singing softly, like a boat.

The spider's web, a delicate lace,
Glistens softly in a sunbeam's grace.
Dewdrops linger, like pearls of light,
Adorning silk in morning's flight.

The winds carry tales from tree to tree,
In the rustling leaves, a mystery.
Roots interlace beneath the ground,
Binding all life in circles profound.

In every creature, in every sound,
A tapestry of life is found.
Colors burst in a dance so free,
Threads of nature, a harmony.

As dusk descends and stars appear,
Nature whispers, calm and clear.
In the silken dance, forever sway,
Threads of magic lead the way.

Harbingers of the Harvest Moon

When autumn's breath begins to chill,
The harvest moon casts shadows still.
Crops gleam golden in its light,
As day surrenders unto night.

The fields are filled with bounteous treasures,
Each ear of corn holds nature's measures.
The earth provides, the sky bestows,
Harbingers of the season's prose.

As lanterns glow in evening's hush,
Creatures stir in a gentle rush.
The call of owls, the rustling leaves,
Speak of harvest, what nature weaves.

In this moment, the world holds breath,
Celebrating life, honoring death.
Thankful hearts gather 'round the food,
Embracing warmth, reflecting mood.

Under the moon's watchful gaze,
Time slows down in its silver blaze.
Beneath its glow, we find our tune,
As we dance in the harvest moon.

Wistful Whispers Through the Threshing

In fields where golden grains do sway,
The whispers of the wind convey.
Soft secrets held in twilight's grasp,
Where time's embrace bids us to clasp.

Beneath the moon's pale, gentle light,
Shadows dance in the still of night.
Each rustle brings a tale to weave,
In the heart of dusk, we believe.

The crickets sing their low refrain,
As starlit dreams begin to reign.
With each sigh, the night unfolds,
A tapestry of stories old.

The sighing trees lean in to hear,
The echoes of a world so near.
In every glimmer, hope ignites,
And whispers spin in silvered lights.

So linger here in nature's thrall,
Where every glance unveils it all.
In wistful whispers, spirits dance,
An age-old tale, a fleeting chance.

Rune of the Sylvan Shadows

In the hush of the woodland's maze,
Ancient runes flicker like fireflies blaze.
The shadows twist and weave a spell,
In this ethereal realm where secrets dwell.

Beneath the boughs so thick and old,
Soft stories of the forest unfold.
With gentle grace, the branches bow,
As if to honor an unseen vow.

Through tangled vines and mossy stone,
A symphony of whispers is grown.
Each rustling leaf, a pulse of lore,
A unity in nature's core.

As twilight settles, dusk becomes,
The stage where magic softly hums.
In every shadow, every gleam,
Resides the heart of a wild dream.

So heed the rhythm, join the song,
In sylvan depths where we belong.
Follow the runes, let courage flow,
For shadows hold the truth we know.

Dewdrops and Distant Lullabies

In morning's grace, the dewdrops gleam,
A crystal world, a gentle dream.
Each droplet sings a lullaby,
Beneath the vast and waking sky.

The flowers yield their softest glow,
As whispers of the dawn bestow.
With petals bright, they join the dance,
In harmony, they find their chance.

The breeze carries secrets from afar,
Echoing dreams of each twinkling star.
A symphony of nature's heart,
In every note, a brand-new start.

The sun peeks through with golden rays,
A tender muse for sunlit days.
In each corner, life starts anew,
In dewdrops, the world's magic brews.

So pause awhile in morning's grace,
In every moment, find your place.
For lullabies in nature's hand,
Hold the tapestry of our land.

The Ballet of the Blossoming Night

Beneath the stars, the night does bloom,
A ballet spun in midnight's room.
With every pause, the world takes flight,
In twirls of silk, the dark feels light.

The moonbeam dancers glide with ease,
Caressing blooms upon the breeze.
Each petal's blush, a tale of grace,
Awakens dreams in this enchanted space.

The owl's soft call, a haunting tune,
Guides the heart beneath the moon.
In shadows deep, the whispers soar,
A choreography forevermore.

As fireflies weave through leafy bower,
They light the stage, they sprinkle power.
Each flicker breathes a wordless song,
In this ballet where hearts belong.

So let the night your spirit lift,
In every movement, find the gift.
For in the bloom of dusk's delight,
We dance together, hearts alight.

Shimmering Veils of Golden Dreams

In twilight's glow, the stars take flight,
Whispers of magic dance through the night.
A tapestry woven, in shimmering threads,
Carrying secrets, where hope gently spreads.

Silver moonlight paints the sky,
While sleepy shadows softly sigh.
Golden dreams in a calm embrace,
Guide our hearts to a wondrous place.

Through forest paths where fairies leap,
Nestled in dreams, the world is deep.
Glowing lanterns flicker and beam,
Leading us forth to a world supreme.

In every heartbeat, the story sways,
As starlit visions steal us away.
A symphony plays in the gentle breeze,
Wrapping our souls in warm melodies.

Tomorrow awaits, with light anew,
Where shimmering veils hold promises true.
So close your eyes, let your worries cease,
And wander the realms of blissful peace.

The Scent of Amber Lullabies

In mellow dusk, a fragrance sweet,
Amber lullabies gently meet.
Notes of solace in the air,
Carry our dreams without a care.

Through fields of gold, the shadows play,
As twilight whispers, drifting away.
Night's embrace wraps around tight,
Swaying to rhythms of soft starlight.

Songs of comfort float on high,
Under the vast, comforting sky.
Every moment painted warm,
In the glow of dreams, we transform.

The lanterns flicker, shadows blend,
Time itself doesn't need to end.
In the scent of amber, hope ignites,
Guiding us softly into the nights.

With every sigh, the world unfolds,
As stories of old begin to be told.
Embrace the magic, the gentle tide,
In amber lullabies, we will abide.

Beneath the Gilded Horizon

Beneath the sunlit skies so bright,
Golden fields stretch, a wondrous sight.
Whispers kiss the gentle breeze,
As dreams sway softly, with such ease.

In twilight's glow, the shadows play,
Painting tales of the fading day.
Each heartbeats rhythm softly sways,
In harmony with nature's maze.

Stars awaken, twinkling bright,
Guiding wanderers through the night.
A tapestry of hope unfurls,
As magic dances through the worlds.

The moonlight bathes the land in grace,
Enchanting all with its embrace.
As dreams and wishes intertwine,
Beneath the sky, forever mine.

To gaze upon the gilded hue,
Is to embrace the life anew.
For every end brings forth a start,
In the realm of the wandering heart.

Reveries of the Harvest Grove

In the grove where whispers dwell,
The amber leaves weave stories well.
Echoes of laughter fill the air,
As nature hums a tune so rare.

Beneath the boughs, the shadows play,
Embracing magic night and day.
With every rustle, dreams take flight,
In harvest's glow, the world ignites.

Golden fruits, a tempting prize,
Nature's bounty, full of surprise.
Each tender stem holds secrets tight,
In twilight's dance, they emerge bright.

With every step, the heartbeats rhyme,
In harmony with the hand of time.
The grove, a refuge from the storm,
Where every spirit finds its form.

So linger long, dear soul, and pause,
For life's sweet beauty earns applause.
In reveries beneath the grove,
There beats a heart, endlessly bold.

Shadows of Delight in the Grain

Among the fields, the shadows creep,
In golden grains, secrets they keep.
A dance of light, a flicker here,
Where laughter mingles with soft cheer.

In every stalk, a tale unfolds,
Of sunlit days and nights so bold.
The breeze while whispers, secrets share,
As dreams take root in open air.

Wanderers tread on paths of gold,
In fields of delight, stories told.
A tapestry of joy and grace,
In nature's arms, we find our place.

With every step, the earth hums sweet,
In shadows where delight and longing meet.
The golden waves roll soft and low,
A symphony of life we know.

So let us dance with carefree hearts,
In fields where every journey starts.
For shadows hold a gentle light,
In grain's embrace, our souls take flight.

A Serenade to the Hidden Spirits

In the quiet glade, where silence sings,
Whispers of magic softly clings.
The trees bow low, their stories told,
As ancient spirits dance, so bold.

Each rustling leaf, a secret shared,
With those who tread and those who dared.
In twilight shadows, echoes soar,
A serenade from days of yore.

Amidst the ferns, where wildflowers bloom,
The air is rich with sweet perfume.
Gentle breezes weave a tune,
As twilight beckons the silver moon.

Come heed the call of the hidden souls,
In each footfall, magic unrolls.
The harmony of hearts entwined,
In nature's breath, true peace we find.

So linger here, beneath the stars,
Where hidden spirits softly are.
In this serenade, we unite,
Together, we embrace the night.

The Faery's Fertile Breath

In twilight's hush, the faeries weave,
Their whispers dance on evening's eve.
With every sigh, the blossoms wake,
Their fragrant dreams in soft light shake.

A gentle pulse, the earth's delight,
Each petal glows in silver light.
They churn the soil, they sing the seeds,
And cradle life where magic leads.

Among the roots, their laughter thrives,
In shadowed groves where nature dives.
With fertile breath, they nurture bold,
The stories in each bud behold.

The nightingale sings, the stars align,
With faery gifts, our hearts entwine.
In every glade, a pulse, a breath,
The life anew, a dance of death.

In moonlit realms, they flit and play,
With woven threads of night and day.
So heed the faery's whispering song,
For in their breath, you do belong.

Mysteries Among the Sheaves

In fields of gold where shadows pool,
There lie the secrets, bright and cruel.
The stalks stand tall, with tales to tell,
Of ancient joys and sorrows' spell.

The wind would dance through bounteous grain,
And lift the whispers of lost pain.
Each sheaf concealed, a tale of yore,
A harvest rich with legends' lore.

Beneath the sun's approving gaze,
The farmer toils in golden haze.
Yet nature's voice, a hushed refrain,
Unfolds the truths that never wane.

Each rustling leaf, each furtive glance,
Invites the heart to take a chance.
For mysteries hide in every stalk,
As time weaves forth its woven clock.

Come, gather 'round, and hear the call,
Of stories in the sheaves that fall.
In every grain, a history seeped,
A world of wonders buried deep.

Glimmers in the Grainfield Glow

In twilight's breath, the fields ignite,
With glimmers caught in soft twilight.
The grainfield waves, an ocean's sigh,
Reflecting dreams that dance on high.

Each stalk pirouettes in gentle breeze,
With whispers sweet that tease and please.
As dusk envelops the earthly sprawl,
A chorus rises, enchanting all.

The fireflies twinkle with youthful glee,
Guiding lost souls through shadowed spree.
They weave their lights 'neath velvet skies,
Where laughter lingers, never dies.

Among the sheaves, the heart sways slow,
To nature's tale in soft aglow.
A symphony beneath the stars,
Where beauty shines and magic's ours.

So linger long in this glowing space,
Feel the pulse of nature's grace.
For in the grainfield's vibrant show,
Life's sweetest moments gently flow.

Tapestry of Nature's Bounty

In every thread, a story spun,
A tapestry where life's begun.
Through verdant arms, both wild and free,
Nature's bounty calls to thee.

The blooms unite, a vibrant feast,
In colors bright, from greatest to least.
Each petal sways with tales of lore,
As bees hum sweetly, longing for more.

The roots entwined with whispers long,
Of ancient rhythms, life's soft song.
In every grain, a promise made,
A legacy that shan't soon fade.

Gather 'round these threads of grace,
Where every being finds its place.
An intricate weave of earth and sky,
Where hopes take flight and souls can fly.

So cherish this tapestry, hold it tight,
For nature's bounty is pure delight.
In every stitch, her heart unfolds,
A boundless treasure, forever holds.

A Tapestry of Sunlit Echoes

In a glade where shadows dance,
Whispers weave through sunny beams,
Each petal catches golden glance,
Nature hums in gentle dreams.

Morning light with silver beams,
Traces paths on twinkling leaves,
Life unfolds in joyful schemes,
Magic stirs as the heart heaves.

Along the brook where ripples play,
Time drifts softly, slow as lace,
Every moment, rich and gay,
Paints the world in warm embrace.

Underneath the elder tree,
Laughter twirls on children's lips,
Spinning tales of what could be,
Holding secrets in their grips.

As dusk falls, the echoes soar,
Sundrops linger, sweet and bright,
Leaving footprints on the floor,
Of a tapestry of light.

Mystical Forms Amongst the Ripe Boughs

In the orchard, shadows twist,
Where apples hang like secrets ripe,
Nature's breath is soft and kissed,
By gales that sing in joyful type.

Branches stretch in emerald hues,
Whispering stories of the vine,
Underneath the sky so blue,
Every knotted root aligns.

With the breeze, a dance unfolds,
Fragrant petals twine and sway,
In the warmth, a dream retold,
Life in bloom, come out to play.

Silhouettes of sprites at dusk,
Flit amongst the boughs with glee,
Chasing after hints of musk,
In this world, let spirits free.

As twilight drapes its velvet sheet,
The orchard softens, hushes deep,
Leaving hearts to feel the beat,
Of magical fruits, secrets keep.

The Scent of Summer's Sorcery

In fields where wildflowers bloom,
Fragrant whispers fill the air,
Colors burst, dispel the gloom,
Spreading joy without a care.

Butterflies in gilded flight,
Dance above the grassy waves,
Chasing sparkles of warm light,
While the sun its gentle saves.

Sunsets drench the sky in gold,
Shadows stretch yet never fight,
Stories of the day unfold,
In the hush of coming night.

Every breeze a tale retells,
Of laughter, love, and fleeting time,
In the garden where magic dwells,
Each moment sings, a perfect rhyme.

The scent of summer, rich and bold,
Calls the dreamers to their muse,
In the warmth, their hearts unfold,
Embracing life, they cannot lose.

Dewdrops Cradling Fables Untold

At dawn, the world is painted bright,
Dewdrops hang on every thread,
Each sparkly gem, a tale in sight,
Whispers of dreams that softly spread.

Hushed moments wrapped in silence,
Nature stirs beneath the sun,
Every blade a sweet defiance,
Of endings and beginnings spun.

Listen close to morning's breath,
As secrets trickle down the leaves,
Life anew, defying death,
In the hush, the spirit believes.

With the sun, the stories rise,
Fables cradle soft and warm,
Through the mist, the laughter flies,
In the heart, a soothing charm.

Underneath the sky so wide,
Dewdrops cradle every glance,
Every drop a chance to bide,
A timeless, twinkling dance.

Whirlwinds of Wonder in the Grain

Golden heads bow low in the breeze,
Whispers of secrets in rustling leaves.
A dance of shadows beneath the sun,
In fields of wonder, we become one.

The sky is a canvas, swirling and bright,
Each grain a story, a spark of delight.
Footsteps of wanderers, lost in the glow,
The heart of the harvest, a soft, gentle flow.

Waves of adventure in every sweep,
Promises whispered in dreams, they seep.
Embrace the wonder, let worries unfold,
In the dance of the grain, stories are told.

With laughter and love, we tread on this land,
Amongst the enchantments, together we stand.
In the heartbeat of nature, we find our refrain,
Life's rhapsody echoes in whirlwinds of grain.

So linger awhile in this magical place,
Where every turn grants a moment of grace.
The world spins in circles, a sweet, tender spin,
In the whirlwinds of wonder, let joy live within.

Constellations Over the Chamomile

Beneath the stars, where the chamomile sighs,
Dreams dance like fireflies in evening skies.
Each flower a wish, a flicker of light,
Constellations weave magic through the night.

The moon hangs low, a silver embrace,
Guiding lost hearts to their destined place.
In laughter and chatter, our spirits align,
Amongst buzzing whispers of sweet, wild thyme.

Dewdrops shimmer like diamonds so bright,
Crickets lull dreams in the hush of the night.
In the night's gentle arms, we spin tales anew,
While constellations gleam in a velvet hue.

Soft petals unfurl with the dawn's first sigh,
Gentle reminders that joys never die.
With each step we take on this winding road,
The stars are our guides, in their light, we're bestowed.

Let the chamomile sway in the cool morning air,
As laughter and love come to intertwine there.
In gardens of stars, where our dreams reconnect,
We'll dance with the cosmos, let our spirits reflect.

The Rhapsody of Lost Agleams

In shadows of twilight, echoes arise,
Whispers of dreams fade into the skies.
Lost agleams of moments, they shimmer and twirl,
Stories forgotten in the heart of the whirl.

Memories shimmer like dew on the grass,
Glimmers of laughter in moments that pass.
In twilight's embrace, we gather the dreams,
Weaving together our rhapsody schemes.

Each sigh of the night holds a secret so dear,
In the silence, we listen, the past lingers near.
With hearts intertwined, we chase what has flown,
In the rhapsody of lost agleams, we've grown.

Underneath starlit skies, we find our way back,
Rekindling memories from shadows we track.
For each lost agleam is a treasure we find,
In the dance of our lives, love's never maligned.

So let them not fade, these agleams of the past,
In the tapestry woven, our stitches hold fast.
With laughter and joy, as our guiding light,
We embrace the sweet echoes that sparkle in night.

Laughter Beneath the Grain Scape

In fields of gold, we frolic and play,
Laughter like ripples in the sun's warm ray.
Beneath the grain scape, joy fills the air,
A tapestry woven with love and with care.

We run through the stalks, wild and free,
Haunted by whispers of dreams yet to be.
Sun-kissed horizons beckon us near,
In moments of mirth, the heart holds no fear.

The breeze carries stories from times long ago,
Of souls who found solace in the undertow.
In hiccups of laughter, our spirits ignite,
As shadows dance softly in fading daylight.

With every soft rustle, a memory gleams,
We craft our own magic, intertwining our dreams.
In the heart of the harvest, our laughter will stay,
A melody cherished in the grain's gentle sway.

So linger awhile in this woven embrace,
Where laughter and hope fill the empty space.
As we journey together, hearts joined like a chain,
In the laughter beneath the grain, love shall remain.

Whispers of Harvest at Twilight

As daylight ebbs, the shadows creep,
In fields where secrets softly sleep.
Golden grains sway in the dusky light,
Whispers of harvest in the night.

The moon's ascent, a silver key,
Unlocks the stories of you and me.
With every breeze, the tales unwind,
Of autumn's gifts that nature's kind.

A tapestry of amber hues,
Beneath the sky, a canvas moves.
The rustling leaves, like voices call,
In twilight's realm, we hear them all.

Hand in hand, beneath the trees,
We stand embraced by evening's breeze.
The dance of shadows all around,
In this stillness, dreams abound.

So let us gather all our fear,
Embrace the magic drawing near.
For in the harvest's gentle sway,
We find our hope at end of day.

A Dance of Dust and Dreams

In the sunlight's warm embrace,
Dust dances through the open space.
Each particle, a spark of light,
A dream ignited, taking flight.

Footsteps echo on the ground,
Life in motion, all around.
The world spins in joyous sway,
As dreams and dust together play.

Whispers drift on fragrant air,
Tales of longing, hearts laid bare.
In fields where hopes begin to bloom,
The dance of dust dispels the gloom.

With every twirl, the past unfolds,
Stories woven, treasures told.
In this moment, pure and bright,
We join the dance into the night.

So let the dust, with dreams entwined,
Guide our spirits, free our minds.
For in this union, we shall find,
The melody of hearts combined.

Secrets of the Golden Meadow

In the meadow, wild and free,
Golden threads of history.
Whispers carried by the breeze,
Secrets nestled in the trees.

Each bloom hides a tale so sweet,
Of whispered loves and chanceful meet.
As twilight paints the sky aglow,
Ancient stories dance below.

A silver brook flows soft and clear,
It hums the songs of yesteryear.
With every stone and bent down blade,
Memories linger, never fade.

The fireflies flicker, stars appear,
In the quiet, dreams draw near.
With every step, the earth does sigh,
For in this place, our spirits fly.

So let us wander, hand in hand,
Through golden fields of ancient land.
For every secret, every dream,
Is woven here, in nature's seam.

Enchantment in the Grain

Waves of amber stretch afar,
Underneath the evening star.
The grain glimmers, soft and sweet,
A magical world beneath our feet.

In this realm where shadows play,
Fables rise with the dying day.
With every rustle, tales unfold,
Of timeless magic, dreams retold.

The dusk brings a soft embrace,
As we wander, lost in space.
Between the stalks, we hear the call,
Of ancient voices, echoing all.

With gentle hands, we touch the earth,
And feel the pulse of nature's birth.
In every seed, a journey lies,
A silent promise beneath the skies.

So let the grain enchant our hearts,
And weave a world where dreaming starts.
For in this space, both wild and free,
We find the magic meant to be.

Fables of the Sunlit Vale

In the vale where sunlight gleams,
Whispers weave enchanting dreams.
Woodland creatures, wise and old,
Guard their secrets, bright and bold.

Butterflies flit in joyous flight,
Painting colors, pure delight.
Beneath the branches, stories spun,
Of love and laughter, lost but won.

Rivers hum a gentle tune,
Beneath the watchful gaze of moon.
Every stone a tale to tell,
A magic woven, all is well.

The flowers bloom with vibrant grace,
In this untouched, wondrous place.
Their fragrance lingers, soft and sweet,
Where earth and sky in union meet.

So gather 'round, oh friends of mine,
Let's share our hearts, let spirits shine.
In Sunlit Vale, our fables bloom,
With every promise, chase the gloom.

The Golden Thread of Magic

A thread of gold in twilight spun,
Weaves together, moon and sun.
It glimmers in the evening air,
A promise of enchantment rare.

In every heart, some magic lies,
Invisible to searching eyes.
But when the dawn begins to break,
Awaken dreams, the world will shake.

Tales of wonder take their flight,
Starlit paths through endless night.
With each new step, adventures grow,
In every heart, let courage flow.

So follow threads with gentle care,
Let warmth and kindness fill the air.
For in the weave, the world unites,
In golden bonds, we find our lights.

Through valleys deep and mountains tall,
Together, we will rise, not fall.
A tapestry of lives entwined,
In magic's clasp, our fates aligned.

Withered Petals in the Breeze

Once vibrant blooms now softly fade,
In time's embrace, their colors jade.
Yet whispers of the past remain,
In withered petals, joy and pain.

The garden softly sighs at dusk,
As shadows wrap the blooms in husk.
Each petal tells a tale once bright,
Of love, laughter, and pure delight.

But life renews with every season,
Each fallen petal holds a reason.
For in decay, the earth will find,
New seeds of hope, the heart entwined.

Embrace the beauty of the ending,
In every loss, a new beginning.
With gentle hands, we'll clear the way,
For future blooms to greet the day.

So let us dance, though petals fade,
In memories where dreams are laid.
For even in the breeze that sweeps,
The heart still holds what softly weeps.

Dance of the Windblown Spirits

Whispers float through evening air,
Spirits dance without a care.
In moonlit glades, where shadows play,
They twirl and weave, come what may.

With laughter soft as gentle sighs,
They swirl beneath the starry skies.
Each fleeting step, a story shared,
In every heartbeat, love declared.

Through forests deep and meadows wide,
In every breeze, they take their ride.
With echoes of the past they play,
Unseen, yet felt in every way.

So close your eyes and you may feel,
The warmth of spirits made of steel.
For in the dance, they find their peace,
In wind and stars, their joy's release.

Embrace the night, let shadows guide,
The windblown spirits by your side.
For in their dance, a promise sings,
Of timeless love and wondrous things.

Faery Footprints in Mossy Nooks

In the hush of twilight's glow,
Whispers of magic ebb and flow.
Tiny prints in emerald strands,
Lead us to enchanted lands.

Beneath the boughs where secrets dwell,
A flicker of light, a silver bell.
Woven dreams in the soft, cool breeze,
Mossy nooks hide mysteries with ease.

Dances shimmering on dew-kissed leaves,
Stories shared that the forest weaves.
Glimmers of laughter, a gossamer trace,
In twilight's arms, we find their grace.

While shadows gather, the night takes flight,
Faery folk twirl under the moon's soft light.
With each fresh step, the magic grows,
In the forest deep, where no one knows.

So wander long where the wild things play,
And follow the footprints, let them lead the way.
For in every nook where the green moss lies,
The heart of the fae gently resides.

Fragments of Forgotten Seasons

Whispers of spring in a gentle sigh,
Faded petals beneath the sky.
Time's embrace cradled soft and tight,
Memories dance in the depth of night.

Autumn leaves fall in a swirling throng,
Echoes of laughter where we belong.
Golden hues paint the edges of dreams,
Moments fade like forgotten streams.

Winter's breath wraps the world in white,
Silence drips like stars in flight.
Frost-kissed whispers of stories untold,
Held in the warmth of hearts so bold.

Scattered fragments of days gone by,
Like sunbeams caught in a clouded sky.
Each fleeting season a treasure bestowed,
Carved in the fabric of the road.

So gather the tales from the winds that blow,
In twilight's embrace, let the fragments flow.
For in the heart of time's gentle stream,
We are the weavers of all that we dream.

The Heartbeat of Wildflowers, Pulsing

In fields where wildflowers breathe and sway,
Their colors pulse in a bright ballet.
Every blossom tells a story true,
Of sunlit mornings and skies so blue.

The gentle rustle of petals in flight,
A melody woven in soft twilight.
Bees buzz in rhythm, a sweet delight,
While whispers of nature embrace the night.

Echoes of laughter from the meadows rise,
In each flower's heart, a dream softly lies.
Petal by petal, the tapestry grows,
In the dance of the wild, the wildflower glows.

With every breath, the earth sings its song,
And through them all, we find where we belong.
In the pulse of the blooms, life comes alive,
A heartbeat of wild where wonders thrive.

So wander through gardens of vibrant hues,
Feel the heartbeat beneath morning's dews.
For in wildflower orchards, love intertwines,
As nature and spirit share secret signs.

Meadow-Lark's Lament

High above the rolling fields,
The meadow-lark's song gently yields.
Soft notes carried on the breeze,
A tale of longing, a heart that pleads.

In golden hours, where shadows play,
Her voice weaves through the end of day.
A symphony born of dusk and dawn,
Threads of sorrow linger on.

Perched on a branch, she sings her heart,
Of lost companions who drift apart.
Each note a tear, each chirp a sigh,
In the twilight, love waves goodbye.

Yet through the pain, a beauty shines,
In melodies formed from tangled lines.
For every end is a new refrain,
The meadow-lark soars free again.

With twilight's kiss upon her plume,
She lifts her voice to dispel the gloom.
In every lilt, hope gently lands,
As the meadow-lark makes new demands.

Driftwood and Dandelion Wishes

Upon the shore where whispers play,
Driftwood gathers in sun's warm sway.
Dandelions dance with the breeze so light,
Wishes float upwards, taking flight.

Each seed a dream, each wave a sigh,
The ocean hums a lullaby.
Nature's scribble on sand and stone,
A canvas where magic feels at home.

Among the shadows, stories twine,
In every grain, a tale divine.
The heartbeat of earth beneath our feet,
This transient place feels bittersweet.

Moments like tides ebb and flow,
Memory's driftwood shaped by woe.
Yet in the light of a fading day,
Hope blooms bright in a gentle way.

With each soft breeze, I close my eyes,
Listening to the ancient sighs.
Dandelion wishes, driftwood dreams,
Life's sweetest magic in fleeting gleams.

The Gossamer Touch of Twilight

As daylight gives in to evening's grace,
A gossamer veil begins to embrace.
Stars twinkle softly, a twinkling delight,
While shadows unfurl in the arms of night.

With whispers of dusk, the world holds its breath,
Holding both life and the promise of death.
Moonlight bathes the landscape in silver sheen,
Awakening secrets that once lay unseen.

In this quiet hour, when dreams take flight,
We gather wishes, igniting the night.
The air heavy with stories unspun,
Each heartbeat echoes, in rhythm with one.

A gossamer thread binds the souls who roam,
In twilight's embrace, we feel most at home.
Let the light linger, let the shadows play,
As we chase the whispers of the closing day.

With every sigh, the stars come alive,
A tapestry woven for those who believe.
In the gossamer touch of this fleeting hour,
We find our solace, we find our power.

Dreams of Honey and Harvest

In fields of gold where the sunbeams gleam,
Dreams entwine with the honeyed stream.
Harvest whispers in the rustling leaves,
A bountiful promise that nature weaves.

From blossoms to fruit, the cycle's embrace,
Time dances slowly in this sacred space.
The sweetness of life, a nectar unknown,
In every heartbeat, our love has grown.

Golden grains that sway in the air,
Threads of richness, beyond compare.
In laughter and toil, we gather and share,
The heart of the earth cradled in care.

With every season, our spirits entwine,
In dreams of honey, both yours and mine.
Together we stand, through storm and through shine,
Bound by our hopes, our hearts intertwine.

In the quiet of dusk, the harvest begins,
A symphony conjured, the melody spins.
Dreams woven gently, a tapestry bright,
In the heart of the fields, we claim our light.

Moonlit Timbers in Bloom

Beneath the moon's watchful, silvery gaze,
Timbers sigh softly, lost in a haze.
In the forest's embrace, the shadows extend,
Where secrets of nature whisper and blend.

Branches like fingers weave tales of old,
In a world where magic, like fireflies, is bold.
The scent of the earth, rich and profound,
Calls forth the dreams from deep underground.

As blossoms unfold in the cool of the night,
Their fragrance entwines in the soft, gentle light.
Moonlit petals, delicate as sighs,
Awaken the magic that deep within lies.

With each passing breeze, the timbers sigh sweet,
In a dance with the night, a rhythm, a beat.
The forest alive, a canvas so wide,
Where hope blooms eternal and secrets abide.

In moonlit lucid dreams, we roam and we play,
Finding solace beneath the night's gentle sway.
Timbers in bloom, under celestial dome,
In nature's embrace, we have finally come home.

Myths Whispered on the Wind

In the hush of twilight's bow,
Legends dance, soft and low.
Whispers wrapped in twilight's song,
Echo stories, where dreams belong.

Stars align in a dusky embrace,
Carrying tales through time and space.
Gentle breezes weave the lore,
Of ancient beings, forevermore.

A fox with eyes of liquid night,
Guides the seekers towards the light.
Each heartbeat shared with the sky,
Hints of truth in every sigh.

Underneath a veil of starlit grace,
Journeying souls find their place.
A secret shared, a whispered vow,
A tapestry woven, here and now.

Through the ages, shadows bloom,
As twilight's call dispels the gloom.
Myths take flight, on wings of breeze,
Where hearts find rest among the trees.

Harmony Beneath the Golden Canopy

In the heart of the emerald glade,
Golden beams form a gentle parade.
Nature's orchestra plays soft and sweet,
Under branches where spirits meet.

Birdsongs echo through lush air,
Filling spaces, light as a prayer.
Leaves sway lightly in sun's embrace,
In this sacred, timeless place.

Beneath the canopy's warm glow,
Cascading dreams in ebb and flow.
Each petal's fall, a silent song,
Reminding us where we belong.

Butterflies flutter, and shadows twirl,
Dancing softly, a magical whirl.
Harmony sings, wrapped in delight,
Beneath the canopy, day turns to night.

With every breath, connection grows,
In the wild where the river flows.
Hand in hand, we walk in peace,
In harmony, our souls find ease.

Fae Secrets of the Field's Edge

Whispers linger in evening light,
Secrets spun with pure delight.
Where daisies bloom, the fae appear,
In laughter lost, yet ever near.

Beneath the boughs of ancient trees,
Fleeting glimpses float on the breeze.
Curled leaves cradle the hidden song,
Echoing where the fae belong.

Tiny lanterns flicker and gleam,
Guiding wanderers who dare to dream.
On soft green beds where wishes hide,
Eldritch magic cannot abide.

In moonlit realms, where shadows play,
Fae coyly beckon, inviting stay.
With every twirl, enchantments weave,
In whispered realms, we believe.

Through dewdrops' gaze and starlit sighs,
The secrets of the fields arise.
In heartbeats swift, they dance and spin,
Drawing us closer, where dreams begin.

The Veil of the Verdant Dreamscape

In whispers woven with soft grass,
Secrets murmur as hours pass.
Where dreams take root in the twilight's fold,
Stories linger, waiting to be told.

A tapestry of green and gold,
Hides the mysteries, old and bold.
Gentle streams in silence flow,
Past the places the dreamers know.

Moonbeams scatter on the forest floor,
As shadows gather and softly roar.
A veil of enchantment cloaks the night,
Inviting souls to take their flight.

Each rustling leaf, a gentle sigh,
A promise made beneath the sky.
The dreamscape breathes in quiet thought,
Embracing all that time forgot.

With every heartbeat, the world expands,
Connecting dreams through tender hands.
In this realm, all fears dissolve,
As the verdant veil begins to evolve.

Where Muses and Meadows Meet

In fields where wildflowers gently sway,
A whisper of dreams begins to play.
The sun dips low, painting skies so bright,
With colors that dance in the fading light.

Muses wander through the golden glade,
Inspiring tales in the twilight's shade.
Laughter echoes, carried on the breeze,
As hearts awaken like the buzzing bees.

With every footstep on the soft, green grass,
The world fades away, and moments pass.
A harmony blooms in the tranquil air,
As wonder lingers, free from all care.

Crisp whispers of evening fill the sky,
Stars begin twinkling, daring to fly.
In this spellbound place, where dreams can roam,
The muses and meadows feel like home.

So let your spirit twirl and spin,
Where the magic of nature can always begin.
In every pause, listen close, you may find,
The muses have woven their magic, entwined.

The Sylph's Silken Serenade

Among the leaves, a soft voice calls,
A sylph flits through the dusk-lit halls.
Her laughter mingles with a gentle sigh,
As stars awaken in the velvet sky.

Her wings, like gossamer, shimmer and glow,
With whispers of secrets no one must know.
In twilight's embrace, she begins to sing,
A timeless tune that makes the heart spring.

Fresh melodies ride on the twilight air,
Entwined with dreams, light as a prayer.
The night listens with a tender ear,
To the serenade only the brave can hear.

Beneath the moon's gaze, her notes take flight,
Carrying hopes into the depth of night.
In every shadow, she weaves her art,
Crafting silken echoes to mend every heart.

So close your eyes and let her draw near,
Feel the warmth of magic, free from all fear.
For in her song, every soul can find,
A whisper of joy in the quiet of mind.

Echoes of the Harvest Moon

The harvest moon rises, large and round,
Casting a glow on the patchwork ground.
Fields of gold in the silver light,
Hold stories whispered through the night.

With each bright ray, shadows come alive,
As crickets sing and the night creatures thrive.
A symphony plays in the cool evening air,
Echoes of joy, beyond all despair.

Corn stalks sway in a rhythmic dance,
As farmers rejoice in the moon's sweet glance.
The world celebrates in this bountiful place,
Harvesting dreams, infused with grace.

Wisps of laughter escape from the fields,
As hearts find solace in what nature yields.
This night draws close with its gentle embrace,
A tapestry woven of time and space.

So gather 'round, share your tales anew,
Under the moon's gaze, bathed in dew.
For in the echoes, the past is spun,
And under the harvest moon, all hearts are one.

Beneath the Starlit Rye

Beneath the starlit rye, dreams take flight,
Whispers of magic awaken the night.
In the golden waves, the shadows play,
As night holds secrets and leads us astray.

The soft wind weaves through each silken stalk,
A gentle melody that hums with talk.
Where wishes are scattered beneath moon's glow,
And in every breeze, there's a tale to sow.

The horizon blushes, kissed by the stars,
As hearts beat in rhythm with distant guitars.
In the quiet of dusk, hopes begin to pry,
Free spirits dance in the starlit rye.

Laughter entwines like vines in the air,
Awakening magic, unaware and rare.
As shadows form stories, old and new,
Beneath the starlit rye, dreams swim through.

So linger a while, and let your soul roam,
Through fields of the night, you'll wander home.
For in every heartbeat, a tale waits,
Beneath the starlit rye, where magic creates.

Candlelight on the Grainy Horizon

In twilight's glow, a flicker bright,
Soft whispers dance, weave through the night.
Shadows weave tales on the scattered sand,
A flicker of hope, in a darkened land.

The horizon glows with dreams untold,
Where magic flares, brave and bold.
With wands of light, the stars join in,
As joy ignites where the night begins.

Faint echoes rise, from the hearth aglow,
Where secrets breathe, and spirits flow.
A canvas painted with flickering rays,
Candlelight guides through life's winding maze.

Threads of silence wrap the glen,
While hearts embrace the gentle zen.
Each spark a whisper, a silent wish,
In candlelight, the moments swish.

So let the light dance, let shadows play,
For in this warmth, fears fade away.
Together we'll journey, hand in hand,
Chasing the glow on this grainy strand.

Songs of the Feathered Kin

In the early morn, where breezes sigh,
Soft feathers flutter, 'neath the azure sky.
Chirps and tweets in a rhythmic play,
As nature welcomes the dawning day.

From branches high, their melodies rise,
A chorus of life, where freedom lies.
Each note a story, tales of the wild,
In harmony shared, like a dreaming child.

With every gentle flit and flight,
They paint the air, a pure delight.
Songs of the feathered, brave and true,
A symphony woven in shades of blue.

In glades and branches, their laughter rings,
A legacy born on the strength of wings.
Together they soar, in a playful spin,
A dance of joy, where life begins.

So listen close, let your heart be still,
For the songs of kin, our spirits fill.
In every chirp, a world unfolds,
The magic of nature, in tales retold.

Harvesting Tales from the Glade

In the heart of the woods, where whispers breathe,
Lie stories hidden, beneath the leaves.
An ancient oak, stands proud and tall,
Keeper of secrets, who hears us all.

With every sigh of the swaying trees,
The past entwines with the gentle breeze.
Footsteps echo on the mossy ground,
As legends awaken, quietly found.

Beneath the moon's soft, silver gaze,
We gather the tales of forgotten days.
Where shadows move, and spirits dance,
In the glow of night, we take our chance.

Berries ripe, with stories to share,
Nature's bounty, our hearts laid bare.
Collecting the whispers, we weave and spin,
Harvesting dreams where all begins.

So come, dear friend, through the hidden glen,
Join the harvest, again and again.
For every tale, like fireflies glow,
Illuminating paths we long to know.

The Weft and Warp of Woodland Wishes

In the loom of night, where shadows weave,
Woodland wishes like dreams conceive.
Threaded in starlight, softly spun,
Each whisper a promise, each heart as one.

Beneath the arch of the silver trees,
Wishes whisper in the rustling breeze.
With gentle hands, we gather the threads,
Tapestries rich, where the magic spreads.

Moonlit paths guide us where we roam,
In the weft and warp, we find our home.
Echoes of laughter, a soft embrace,
In every corner, we find our place.

The night is alive with secrets untold,
In the woodland's heart, where dreams unfold.
So come, dear friend, let our wishes soar,
In the fabric of night, we'll forever explore.

With every stitch, our hopes combine,
In the magic of friendship, our souls align.
The weft and warp in harmony sing,
Binding our hearts in the joy we bring.